SHORT BOOK OF OPTIMIZ

I0014867

MAHINROOP PM

PRINTED AND PUBLISHED BY AMAZON

PRICE

EBOOK: $6

PAPERBACK: $13

Introduction

'Short Book of Search Engine Optimization' is a comprehensive book on search engine optimization. Both beginner and advanced internet marketers can get benefitted from the book 'Short Book of Search Engine Optimization'. This book is written in a format that flows easily and readers can get an encompassing picture of Search Engine Optimization through the book 'Short Book of Search Engine Optimization'. List of topics covered in the book include introduction to search engine optimization, advanced search engine optimization, Amazon search engine optimization, best search engine optimization plug-ins for WordPress, best search engine optimization software and blog search engine optimization.

About the Author

MAHINROOP PM is an Information Technology consultant based in India. The author is passionate about technology, ecommerce, websites and books. He has published four books entitled as 'Mega Book of Website Designing', 'Blogging Masterclass Package 2018', 'Big Book of Vatakara' and 'Web Marketing Super Course' respectively.

Written by MAHINROOP PM

Table of Contents

Introduction to search engine optimization

Advanced search engine optimization

Advantages of search engine optimization

Amazon search engine optimization

Basics of search engine optimization

Best books on search engine optimization

Best search engine optimization plug-ins for WordPress

Best search engine optimization software

Blog search engine optimization

Career in search engine optimization

Content marketing and search engine optimization

Google search engine optimization

How to do search engine optimization?

Joomla search engine optimization

Local search engine optimization

On page search engine optimization

Off page search engine optimization

Difference between search engine optimization and search engine marketing

Keyword research

Search engine optimization ranking factors

Introduction to Search Engine Optimization

Search Engine Optimization is a set of practices used for optimising a website for increased visibility in search engine result pages. The basic principles of SEO (Search Engine Optimization) are clear and easy to understand. Search engine optimization is absolutely essential for building a successful web presence and SEO is interrelated with usability in website designing. According to web marketing maestros, the end result of SEO is a highly visible, easily navigable and accessible website. A website needs to be properly optimized in order to get top rank in a search engine and SEO should be continually monitored.

SEO is helpful in maximising the number of visitors to a website and search engine optimization is often about making small modifications to a website. Search engine optimization has big impact on the user experience of a site and performance in organic results. It should be kept in mind that search engine optimization is more than SEO factors as well as algorithms. No single SEO factor will provide top rankings on search engine results pages and SEO is the well balanced combination of research, planning and optimization. The search engine giant Google has over 200 ranking factors and over 10000 sub signals for ranking.

Search engine optimization is important because the majority of web traffic is driven by search engines like Google, Yahoo and Bing. Investing in SEO offers higher return on investment and solid SEO is required to compete online today. Usability of the website is very critical in search engine optimization and SEO is the best tool to drive people to a blog or website. It has been pointed out that the art and science of search engine optimization is not that simple like many of us think. Bloggers, small business owners and internet marketers can benefit from the services provided by SEO consultants.

The world of search engine optimization is constantly changing and the key steps to successful SEO are crawl accessibility, compelling content, optimized keywords, great user experience, share worthy content, and snippet mark-up. Search engine optimization is one of the crucial aspects of web marketing and knowing the basics of SEO is essential to launch a successful web marketing campaign. Great SEO strategy will put a website on top of Google search results and SEO makes a search relevant to the user. SEO plays a key role in driving traffic to a website and titles, headings and links are other prominent SEO ranking factors. Understanding the significance of keyword is important in a SEO strategy and choosing the right keywords can increase SEO ranking.

The key aspects of SEO strategy include links, titles, Meta descriptions, headings, originality of content, videos and images. Search engine optimization is dependent upon content as a whole and the content in a website should sound as natural as possible. The ideal content in a website should be interesting, engaging, fresh, original, short and succinct. Wise usage of keyword, optimized images, great titles, and relevant links are key aspects of search engine optimization. Search engines including Google, Yahoo and Bing love up to date, relevant and interesting content.

The list of key SEO tools includes Google Analytics, Google Webmaster Tools, Google Ads keyword tool, Google Alerts, Google Trends, and Google Page Speed. There are numerous online SEO tools available and some companies hire renowned SEO consultants. SEO is an ongoing process and posting high quality content consistently on website is a key part of search engine optimization strategy. The ultimate goal of search engine optimization is to rank as high as possible for a certain search query. White hat SEO refers to techniques that search engines recommend as a part of good design and they produce long term results. Black hat SEO uses techniques that are disapproved by search engines and websites employing black hat SEO will suffer a ranking penalty.

Content management system, click through rate, Meta tags, organic traffic, search engine results page, spider and user generated content are the important concepts in search engine optimization. Search Engine Optimization is all about search engine rankings and higher ranking equals to higher click through rate. The most important search engine ranking factors are links, keywords, site age, freshness, site speed and site structure. Links from authoritative websites will have more impact than links from less popular websites in SEO. A basic SEO principle is that the keyword should appear in domain, URL, title, header tags, and content.

Google considers old websites as more authoritative than new ones and frequently updating website is an excellent SEO tip. Google Panda and Google Penguin are the most popular search engine algorithms by the tech tycoon Google. Mobile Search Engine Optimization has huge importance since the market of Smartphones and tablets is showing growth trajectory. Optimizing a website for mobile devices has become a must today and responsive design is recommended by Google due to the benefits like reduced loading time.

Elements Weighed by Google's Algorithm

How people engage with the website?

Loading speed of the site

Mobile friendliness of the site

How much unique content the site has?

Domain level keyword features, domain level link authority features, page level link features, page level content features, social metrics, domain level keyword usage and domain level brand features are key components of Google SEO strategy. The title tag of a website should be of 55-60 characters and Google prefers long form content in websites. It has been reported that organic traffic converts better than paid traffic and SEO has become very competitive today. Blogging is a leading source of leads and search engine optimization ensures that blog posts get found. Content marketing is the vital part of search engine optimization strategy and the content in the company website needs to be engaging.

Search engine marketing is incredibly important for internet marketers and blogging is very helpful in boosting SEO. Google Ads Keyword Tool and SEM Rush are the best tools to find the keywords related to a blog. Utilizing the keywords throughout the blog post is an excellent SEO tip and keywords can be included in title, headings, sub headings, and introductory sentence. Optimizing the images, giving readers an opportunity to subscribe to the blog and using social media to broaden the reach of blog posts are the best blogging SEO tips. Hootsuite is the best social media management application for blogs and one of the best things to increase search engine optimization is by starting a blog.

Advanced Search Engine Optimization

Completing SEO audit on the website is the first and foremost step of advanced search engine optimization. SEO audit refers to examining overall site performance, setting new goals, and implementing techniques to reach those goals. Internet marketers should ensure that their web pages have Meta descriptions and titles and each page on website is optimized for SEO keywords. Important tips for URL optimization include using readable URLs, using hyphens in URLs, adding mobile URLs to sitemaps, using canonical URLs and uploading a favicon. Advanced SEO focuses on creating valuable content, building high quality links, and prioritizing semantic search.

The mobile site should be prioritized for mobile first indexing and internet marketers should create content keeping mobile in mind. Making short brand videos, creating educational videos, running live broadcasts, and uploading videos to different platforms like YouTube, Facebook and Instagram are some of the advanced search engine optimization techniques. It is an excellent SEO practice to submit video sitemap to search engines and updating the 'Google My Business' listing is another advanced SEO tip. Brand reputation matters in the Google search engine rankings and links are still important in Search Engine Optimization. Google Search Console is an essential SEO tool and its useful features include URL inspection, index coverage report, and performance report.

Listing the products on Amazon is an advanced SEO tip since Amazon is the Google of ecommerce. The Google search algorithm defines relevance by engagement behaviour while the Amazon search algorithm defines relevance by purchase behaviour. Sales velocity is a key factor in Amazon search engine optimization and creating great content is an essential Amazon SEO strategy. Link building is an advanced search engine optimization strategy since it is a reliable method of building long term growth. A quick link building tip is to get links from sites that use visual content without reference and advanced SEO is a set of SEO techniques that requires some degree of expert knowledge.

Advanced SEO includes technical SEO concepts and a broad understanding of Google search algorithm is necessary to master advanced SEO. The advanced search engine optimization takes care of metrics like content, keywords and back links. Writing long blog posts is an advanced search engine optimization technique and it is an essential factor to improve search rankings. According to street smart internet marketing professionals, long form content will help a website to get better SEO rankings. Quality back links are the principal components of advanced SEO and back links are equivalent to reliability for Google. Back links is one of the top rated SEO ranking factors and quality back links can be obtained by guest blogging.

Collaborating with social media influencers is another well known method to get quality back links. The best tools for keyword research are KW Finder, Moz Keyword Explorer, and Google Keyword Planner. Having social media presence on sites like Facebook, Twitter, Instagram and Pinterest will help a website to improve search engine rankings. Writing better headlines is another advanced search engine optimization tactic and using appropriate tags for visual content is another excellent SEO tip. Using more Infographics in posts is another SEO tactic and a website should have mobile friendly design.

Optimizing a website for mobile devices will affect search rankings and improving page loading speed is another advanced SEO technique. Page loading speed is an important ranking factor for desktop searches and optimizing the content for voice searches is another SEO tip. Video content has retention rate than textual content and creating good website architecture is another SEO tactic. Back linking, website speed and quality content are the key pillars of advanced search engine optimization. Some of the key Google search engine ranking factors include leading keywords in H1 tags, leading keywords in H2 tags, search terms in the HTML tag, and search terms in body tag. Writing high quality articles that provide solutions to the real challenges of customers is the key aspect of SEO strategy.

Image slicing and resolution reduction are the key image optimization techniques popular among internet marketers. The content in a website should be broken up with header tags and blogging is great for search engine optimization. Blogging is an outstanding tool for lead generation and improving search engine optimization rankings. Producing fresh, updated and relevant content is quite important as far as search engine optimization is concerned. Outbound links increase the credibility of a website and internal links too are equally important in SEO.

Adding multimedia elements like videos, slideshows and audios will help a website to get higher search engine rankings. It has been reported that there is a correlation between videos and search engine optimization rankings. Content in a website should be written in a way people can understand and fixing the broken links is another SEO strategy. It is necessary to properly format web page and coloured text, bold fonts and italics should be used. Clean format and design of the typical website will be helpful in improving search engine rankings. Providing appropriate contact information in the website is a vital search engine optimization tip. Social sharing buttons should be enabled and businesses should share links on social media platforms.

The key components of Google's ranking algorithm are link popularity of the specific page, trust of the host domain, social graph metrics, traffic, CTR data, on page keyword usage and anchor text of external links to the page. Writing click worthy titles and descriptions is an integral aspect of advanced search engine optimization. Creating clean, optimized and focused URLs is another important search engine optimization tip. Writing a great Meta description is absolutely important and plug-ins like All in One SEO Pack can be used for increasing search engine rankings. According to prominent web marketers, the ideal Meta description in a website should be descriptive, unique as well as short.

Creating a mobile app can boost SEO and it is a great investment although it is known as an expensive option. Latent semantic indexing can give SEO boost and it is the process search engines use to find related keywords in addition to the main keyword. Publishing press releases is another advanced SEO tip and press releases can be featured in premium news sites including ABC, NBC, CBS and Fox News. Local SEO is important for brick and mortar businesses and small businesses can setup an account on Google Business. Getting into the Google News is an excellent SEO tip and the news content should be authoritative.

Advantages of Search Engine Optimization

SEO paves the way towards better user experience and photos, videos and easily navigable websites lead to better user experience. Search engine optimization is the primary source of leads and inbound strategies like content marketing are the successful source of leads. According to web marketing experts, SEO results in higher conversion rate and it promotes better cost management. Search engine optimization lowers advertising costs and inbound lead generation methods like search engine optimization and social media management are cost effective. SEO encourages local customers to visit the nearby physical store after the online research and it builds brand credibility.

Search engine optimization is helpful in establishing brand awareness and SEO ensures that products are easily found by search engine sites. SEO ensures mobile friendliness of a website and mobile friendliness has significant impact on search engine rankings. Search engine optimization is highly effective as a long term marketing strategy and six months is the minimum time to get good search engine rankings. SEO helps a business organization to gain market share and it increases conversion rates to a very large extent. Search engine optimization creates synergy of all marketing activities online and all online marketing strategies will contribute to the success of search engine optimization.

Content marketing, social media marketing and blogging will help a website to get higher search engine rankings. SEO increases followers on social media sites including Facebook, Twitter, Pinterest, Instagram and LinkedIn. It is a well known fact that SEO increases website speed and the website speed can affect search engine rankings. Search engine optimization is a key part of any successful web marketing strategy and SEO has the power to make huge impact on business. One of the best advantages of SEO is that it is an inbound marketing strategy and it is customer centric.

Search engine optimization gets more clicks than pay per click and SEO is helpful in public relations. The biggest connection between search engine optimization and public relations lies in link building. Earning links from reputable websites is an essential SEO strategy and SEO enables a business organization to move ahead in the competition. Small businesses can create robust, user friendly and fast websites that rank higher in search results using SEO. SEO of the contemporary age is about improving the user experience too and effective SEO brings in more customers. Search engine optimization is the most affordable internet marketing strategy of today and businesses with SEO optimized website will grow twice as fast as businesses without SEO optimized website.

It has been reported that Search Engine Optimization will improve the searchability and visibility of a website. Organic search is often the primary source of web traffic and Google owns a very large portion of the search market. The ultimate objective of any search engine optimization campaign is to build trust as well as credibility. Good SEO is equal to better user experience and optimal user experience is an inseparable element of search engine optimization. Local Search Engine Optimization leads to increased engagement, traffic as well as conversions.

Local SEO focuses on optimizing digital properties for specific vicinity and it features specific towns, cities and regions. The local SEO consists of optimizing the brand's website, content, local citations, back links, and local listings. Optimizing 'Google My Business Listing' and social media profiles are key steps involved in local SEO. Local SEO refers to optimizing in sites like Yelp, Home Advisor and Angie's list depending upon the industry. Businesses who want to succeed in the digital space make use of search engine optimization and SEO traffic is highly relevant. It is a well known fact that search engine optimization increases engagement rate and SEO drives more sales. SEO offers long term results and it can be integrated with other internet marketing efforts like content marketing.

One of the key benefits of search engine optimization is that it increases the visibility of a website in search engines. Properly executed SEO can boost organic traffic and it increases the chances of driving more people to the website. One of the biggest benefits of SEO is that it enhances the user experience and it creates an everlasting impression on the audience. SEO involves tactics like developing an easy to navigate layout, optimizing page load speed and using mobile friendly design. The fantastic benefits of SEO include attracting a highly relevant audience to the website and improving user experience.

The benefits of search engine optimization are interconnected and advanced SEO is a springboard of innovative web marketing ideas. Numerous case studies prove that search engine optimization can drive better sales and mobile friendly site with optimized layout simplifies user interactions. Resolving technical issues in the website, changing site architecture, and reorganizing the sitemap are some of the best SEO tips. One of the greatest benefits of SEO is that it can help a business organization to cut costs and it reduces cost per acquisition. A big plus point of search engine optimization is that it is highly measurable and Google Analytics is the best tool to measure the effectiveness of SEO campaign.

SEO impacts public relations initiatives of a business organization and guest blogging is an important search engine optimization strategy. Search Engine Optimization is influenced by content marketing, website designing, and social media marketing. Content marketing features producing high quality content and it is required for search engine optimization too. According to Information Technology experts, effective SEO will result in long term exponential business growth. The ultimate objective of search engine optimization is increasing the conversion rate of a website.

Smaller companies can make their business more visible by using SEO and search engine optimization is beneficial to companies of all sizes. SEO offers the benefits of understanding prospects, improved knowledge of industry and business competition. Search Engine Optimization comes with tangible benefits like new business or referrals and SEO agency can be a great business partner. Effective SEO paves the way towards measurable return on investment and the long term results offered by SEO makes it popular among businesses. SEO is undoubtedly a powerful web marketing strategy and low cost and high return on investment characterise SEO campaign. High page ranks on Google are equal to being a reputable company and SEO can enhance the credibility of a website in different ways. Link building, content optimization and social engagement are some of the best approaches to build a reputable website.

Amazon Search Engine Optimization

It is very important to understand that the search engine of Amazon works differently than the search engine of Google. Amazon is primarily a buying platform and the search algorithm of Amazon is known as A9. According to skilled SEO digerati, the Amazon product page should be optimized for relevance as well as performance. The list of Amazon ranking factors include product title, seller name, Amazon backend keywords, brand, product description, product pricing, Amazon product conversion rate, product image, and Amazon customer reviews. The most important part of Amazon Search Engine Optimization is the product title and relevant keywords should be included in the product title.

Tips to Optimize Amazon Product Name

Include brand name

Mention specific ingredients

Specify the colour of product

Mention the quantity of product

Include a clear description of the product

Companies should avoid keyword stuffing in their Amazon product titles and Amazon marketers should pay attention to seller name. The typical Amazon product description should be detailed and companies selling on Amazon should follow the ecommerce landing page best practices. Amazon product description should contain specifics of the product as well as its vital ingredients. The Amazon product pricing affects the conversion rate and the conversion rate will be positively affected if the product pricing is competitive.

Products that feature high quality images have a better conversion rate in Amazon and Amazon's online reviews are another performance related ranking factor. More reviews in Amazon equal to more sales and having more reviews have an impact on click through rates. Images, titles and backend search terms are three crucial components of Amazon search engine optimization. Internet marketers should keep in mind that Amazon cares about buyers and selling stuff to those buyers. Making products more visible than the products of competitors is an essential Amazon SEO strategy.

The Amazon ranking algorithm A9 is a maturing algorithm and the product listings in Amazon should be properly optimized, clear and appealing to potential customers. Appealing product images, optimized product title, competitive product pricing, and attractive product title are the key Amazon ranking factors. Amazon search algorithm takes into account multiple factors like fulfilment method, price, stock availability, and Amazon keyword research. A typical Amazon product title should incorporate all the relevant information and it should include brand, product, material, quantity and colour. An optimized product title is a very important ranking factor in Amazon and keyword optimization is important in Amazon too. Product price is a vital performance factor in Amazon marketplace and it affects the product purchase.

Product pictures are key sales drivers in Amazon and high definition images should be used in Amazon product descriptions. Amazon recommends using large images in product descriptions and the positive characteristics of the product should be displayed in Amazon product descriptions. The right keywords should be placed in an Amazon product description and presenting the Amazon product description in bullet points is an excellent idea. It is to be ensured that the product never runs out of stock in Amazon as it can lose huge amount of rankings. Product ratings and reviews are integral components of Amazon Search Engine Optimization.

It is to be noted that Amazon continually changes its algorithm and Amazon SEO refers to optimizing product listings to appear on the top of Amazon search results. Optimized product listings in Amazon leads to better ranking and better rankings lead to more visibility. Amazon rankings are the most important factors of business success and the ecommerce giant ranks products based on purchase likelihood. It is a well known fact that keywords and performance determine the rankings in world's biggest ecommerce site. The purchase likelihood in Amazon varies for every search query and performance in Amazon is measured by click through rates and conversion rates.

Amazon search engine optimization helps businesses to reach more customers and the Amazon algorithm focuses on displaying products that increase purchase likelihood. Images play a vital role in the Amazon purchase process and typical product images in Amazon are larger than 1000*1000 pixels. Adding zoomable images in Amazon product description increases conversion rate and sellers should look at the prices offered by competitors. The search algorithm of Amazon is brand agnostic and content relevance to search queries, quality of content, product pricing, product popularity and number of reviews affect Amazon search engine rankings. Sellers should place long tail keywords in the Amazon product description and the right combination of keywords should be used in Amazon product listing.

It is an excellent practice to use attractive and optimized product details in Amazon product description. The details should be kept specific in Amazon product description and keywords should be used naturally in a typical Amazon product description. Images have a big impact on the visibility of product in Amazon and the images should highlight the product from every angle. Amazon allows including videos in product descriptions and positive reviews will increase conversion rates in Amazon. The content in an Amazon product description page should be 100% unique and it is good to having as many links as possible.

The A9 algorithm ranks products based on sales performance history, text match relevance, price and product availability. The list of indirect factors that affect Amazon search engine rankings include fulfilment method, reviews, premium content, advertising and promotions. Optimized product descriptions and product titles help a seller to stand out from the rest in the highly competitive marketplace of Amazon. Products with higher sales will be placed higher upon the Amazon search ranking list and it is essential to create a product listing that will convert. The Amazon product description should be as accurate as possible and a product should have a concise and unique title.

Product title is the first source of information in a typical Amazon product listing and it should have correct capitalization and spelling.

Best Practices for Product Features in Amazon

Highlight the top five features

Begin bullet point with a capital letter

Write in fragments

Write numbers as numerals

Separate phrases in one bullet point with semicolon

Product descriptions in Amazon are few paragraphs long and they may require some light HTML editing. Amazon encourages sellers to include correct dimensions, care instructions and warranty information in product description. Sellers should not include seller name, email address, website URL, and company specific information in Amazon product description.

Basics of Search Engine Optimization

Search engine optimization is the art of publishing information that ranks well in search engines like Google, Yahoo and Bing. SEO consists of different steps including market research, keyword research, on page optimization, site structure, link building, brand building, viral marketing and staying up to date with changes in SEO. Unique and descriptive page titles play a crucial role in successful search engine optimization efforts. Some of the best link building strategies include submitting sites to general directories like DMoz, submitting sites to relevant niche directories, and getting links from industry sites. Paid search is often called as Pay per Click or PPC and Google Ads is the PPC program of Google.

Search engine optimization is all about organic rankings and search engine marketing is the mixture of search engine optimization and pay per click. The search engine marketing includes both organic search engine optimization as well as paid search. Local SEO, on page SEO and off page SEO are different types of search engine optimization strategies. The history of search engine optimization dates back to the 1990s and it has become an essential web marketing strategy today. Search engine optimization is an ever growing industry and SEO is about running the right website for the right people.

High quality and well optimized website content is the most basic requirement of a successful search engine optimization campaign. The SEO success is often dependent upon common sense and few best internet marketing practices. On page SEO refers to optimizing the website to affect the organic search results and Meta tags, headings, URL structure, image optimization, content, structured data, and website speed are key components of on page SEO. Off page SEO includes activities like guest blogging, email outreach, submissions, and cooperation with influencers. White hat SEO focuses on well written content, natural links, brand building, content strategy, on page optimization, keyword research and quality.

Black hat SEO refers to unethical practices to improve rankings in search engine results page and white hat SEO is a long term strategy to improve user experience. Search engines like Google, Yahoo and Bing work by crawling, indexing and selecting the results. The list of critical SEO success factors include well targeted content, crawlable website, quality of links, unique content, fresh content, click through rate and website speed. Some other important SEO ranking factors include use of relevant keywords, HTTPS, link relevance, social sharing, domain age, and page layout. Search queries can be classified into navigational search queries, informational search queries and transactional search queries.

Search engine optimization is about targeting real people and it is an important branch of web marketing. Online shops, blogs, and small businesses can get hugely benefitted from search engine optimization. SEO is divided into two main sections: on page search engine optimization and off page search engine optimization. On page SEO is associated with the content, structure and images of a website and it focuses on structural components. The basic principle of Search Engine Optimization is to create relevant, high quality as well as topic relevant content.

Link building and social signals are two most common aspects of off page search engine optimization. Back link is one of the most important ranking factors in Google and link building is a major part of SEO. Back links are generally used to measure the popularity of a website and quality of the back links is the most important thing as far as off page search engine optimization is concerned. The term link building refers to all efforts to generate back links or to acquire back link partners. Comments under blog article is counted as social signals and some of the most prominent Google search ranking factors include relevance to the search, expertise of the source, trustworthiness of the source and mobile friendliness.

Some of the best SEO tools include Google Search Console, SEM Rush, KW Finder, Yoast SEO, Moz, Spyfu, Screaming Frog, and Fat Rank. Google Search Console is a useful SEO tool which can be used to identify duplicate metadata and number of indexed pages. According to buggy techies, SEM Rush is helpful in assessing present rankings and changes in rankings. The ability to find long tail keywords is an exquisite feature of KW Finder and it is unquestionably a great SEO tool. Yoast SEO is the best SEO plug-in for WordPress and it can be used to optimize Meta tags and content.

Creating SEO friendly content is quite easy with the help of Yoast SEO and Moz is an advanced SEO tool which offers features like keyword recommendations and site crawls. SpyFu is the best search engine optimization tool to rank for particular keywords and Screaming Frog is an incredible SEO tool. The Screaming Frog can be used to fix issues related to content, redirections as well as link building. Ahrefs is an excellent SEO tool for keyword research, rank tracking, competitor analysis and SEO audit. Fat Rank is a free keyword tool which can be used to know the ranking of the keywords and search engine optimization involves creating informational content.

Product page SEO, content SEO, technical SEO, local SEO and voice search SEO are key types of SEO. The focus of product page SEO is on creating original content that fascinates the user and creating content that attracts audience is the key feature of content SEO. Brands can implement different content SEO methods like creating highly shareable content, creating ebooks, and reaching out to influencers. Technical SEO features the back end elements of SEO and it is important in improving search results. Local SEO is important for brands having regional customer base and working on local SEO will help a brand to get more leads.

It is important to optimize the content on web pages for voice search and Ahrefs is the second largest website crawler after Google. Ahrefs is one of the most dependable SEO tools in the universe and it is used to determine the most linked content within a particular niche. The Ahrefs is used for keyword research, rank tracking, competitor analysis, SEO audit, and viral content research. Google Search Console can be used to monitor the web presence in Google Search Engine Results page. SEM Rush has been the favourite marketing tool of web marketers all over the world and it showcases incredible features.

Best Books on Search Engine Optimization

Some of the best books on search engine optimization include 'The Art of SEO: Mastering Search Engine Optimization', 'Search Engine Optimization All in One for Dummies', 'SEO 2017: Learn Search Engine Optimization with Smart Internet Marketing Strategies', 'Marketing in the age of Google' and 'Content Machine: Use Content Marketing to Build A 7 Figure Business with Zero Advertising'. 'The Art of SEO: Mastering Search Engine Optimization' is written by Eric Enge, Stephan Spencer, and Jessie C Stricchiola. It is a must read book on search engine optimization for novice and experienced web marketing professionals. The book features information on search engine basics, SEO planning, SEO implementation, keyword research, website development, content marketing and social media.

'The Art of SEO: Mastering Search Engine Optimization' describes Google algorithms including Google Panda and Google Penguin. It is an in-depth educational book on SEO and the authors share innovative SEO techniques in the book. 'The Art of SEO: Mastering Search Engine Optimization' is an awesome book and it is very easy to understand. The book touches on every aspect of search engine optimization and it is written by polyhistor authors. It features wealth of information on the topic of SEO and the book is perfect for anyone starting to learn SEO.

'Search Engine Optimization All in One for Dummies' is written by Bruce Clay and it is one of the best books on search engine optimization. This book features information on keyword strategy, linking strategy, content, web design, programming, and creating SEO friendly site. The book 'Search Engine Optimization All in One for Dummies' is surely a search engine optimization classic. It is a comprehensive resource on search engine optimization and 'Search Engine Optimization All in One for Dummies' is a fantastic book on SEO. The book covers almost all SEO related topics and it is the book written by SEO legend Bruce Clay.

Both beginner and advanced SEO professionals can make use of the book 'Search Engine Optimization All in One for Dummies'. It has lots of great information on search engine optimization and it is a well organized book. This book will be of great help in learning more about SEO procedures and it gets the basic questions of SEO answered. Readers can learn how search engines work, how to apply effective keyword strategies, ways to position SEO and international SEO through this super book. This book illustrates the instinctual search engine optimization skills of the author equipped with creativity.

The book 'SEO 2017: Learn Search Engine Optimization with Smart Internet Marketing Strategies' is a combo package of creativity plus innovation. This well known book is written by Adam Clarke and the book features info on how Google works, history of SEO and how Google ranks keywords. 'SEO 2017: Learn Search Engine Optimization with Smart Internet Marketing Strategies' focuses on keyword research, on page SEO, link building, social media, website analytics, local SEO and troubleshooting SEO problems. Adam Clarke discusses Google algorithm updates and PPC advertising with Google in the book 'SEO 2017: Learn Search Engine Optimization with Smart Internet Marketing Strategies'.

'SEO 2017: Learn Search Engine Optimization with Smart Internet Marketing Strategies' is a well written book on search engine optimization. Small business owners can get immensely benefitted from the book and it features the SEO best practices. Amazon is flooded with glowing reviews of the book 'SEO 2017: Learn Search Engine Optimization with Smart Internet Marketing Strategies'. It is a detailed reference guide on search engine optimization and individuals setting up a blog can make use of this amazing book. The author has explained hard search engine optimization concepts in a very simple language and it features information on pay per click and analytics.

'Marketing in the age of Google' by Vanessa Fox is a top rated book on search engine optimization. It is written in a very simple language and the author is a leading consultant on search engine strategy. 'Marketing in the Age of Google' is the best book about search engine marketing available today. It is absolutely a must read book for internet marketing professionals and the book covers so much of information about search engine marketing. The book 'Marketing in the Age of Google' fascinates each and every reader and it is written by a humdinger technocrat.

Graphs, pictures and illustrations are used throughout the book 'Marketing in the Age of Google' to explain the concepts clearly. It is an undisputable fact that 'Marketing in the Age of Google' is one of the smartest books on web marketing. This book is about the new era of market research and it is full of helpful ideas as well as useful tips. The book 'Marketing in the Age of Google' is well written and the author explains concepts in plain English. 'Marketing in the Age of Google' will be beneficial to solo entrepreneurs and it is a must read for every information technology professional.

The book 'Content Machine: Use Content Marketing to Build a 7 Figure Business with Zero Advertising' is an excellent resource on content marketing. It covers info such as content marketing basics, high quality content and how to scale the content machine. The book showcases a strategy of content marketing for building a seven figure business with zero advertising. 'Content Machine: Use Content Marketing to Build a 7 Figure Business with Zero Advertising' teaches the fundamentals of content marketing. It showcases best practices in business blogging and the book is full of content marketing tips and strategies.

Simple and easy to follow language make the book 'Content Machine: Use Content Marketing to Build a 7 Figure Business with Zero Advertising' stand out from the rest. The book is a must read for every internet entrepreneur and it is a guide on how to create high quality content based internet business. It is unquestionably one of the best books on content marketing written by a self styled business book author. Useful and actionable information given in the book 'Content Machine: Use Content Marketing to Build a 7 Figure Business with Zero Advertising' makes it popular among internet marketers. The book is power packed with lots of useful information and it is a one stop shop for content marketing.

Best Search Engine Optimization Plug-ins for WordPress

The list of best search engine optimization plug-ins for WordPress include Yoast SEO, SEM Rush, Google Search Console, Ahrefs, Google Keyword Planner, All in One SEO pack and SEO Press. Yoast SEO is a top rated SEO plug-in available in the market and it features a complete website optimization tool. It can be used to add SEO titles and descriptions to posts along with automatically generating XML sitemap. Yoast SEO is one of the most valuable tools for a self hosted WordPress site and it is one of the widely used WordPress plug-in. It is a powerful tool which can make a website as search engine friendly as possible and Yoast can be installed on any self hosted WordPress site.

The premium version of Yoast SEO offers extra functionality and its free version is also feature rich. The Yoast SEO WordPress plug-in takes care of control titles, Meta descriptions, sitemaps and much more. A typical SEO plug-in for WordPress is used for adding social share buttons, getting statistics about shares, checking comments for spam, creating image galleries and optimizing for search. Yoast SEO is a WordPress plug-in designed to make onsite SEO very simple for WordPress users. The Yoast SEO makes SEO simple and no coding knowledge is required to use Yoast SEO plug-in.

SEM Rush is a popular SEO tool used for keyword research, competitor analysis and Google ad campaign optimization. Bloggers use SEM Rush for more traffic and revenue and it is mainly used to find profitable keywords. The best feature of SEM Rush is that it can be used by any number of sites and SEM Rush is used to identify variety of keywords. SEM Rush is one of the most essential search engine marketing tools and it offers a fourteen day free trial. Google Search Console is a collection of tools and resources used by website owners, web masters, web marketers and SEO professionals.

The illustrious features of Google search console include search appearance, search traffic, status updates, and crawling data. Google Search Console was previously known as Google Webmaster Central and it was rebranded as Google Search Console in 2015. The Google Search Console includes viewing referring domains, mobile site performance, rich search results and high traffic queries. Google Search Console is a free tool offered by Google that helps website owners maintain and monitor their website presence. It shows which keywords are the website ranking for, anchor text, average position, and impressions. Yoast SEO comes with an easy integration that lets setting up search console without writing any code.

All in One SEO is a very popular SEO plug-in and it offers comprehensive set of tools to improve a website. This plug-in can be used to add SEO title, Meta tags, open graph Meta tags, XML sitemaps, and image sitemaps. It has been pointed out that All in one SEO comes with easy setup and it gives access to more add-ons. All in one SEO is a more affordable option than Yoast SEO and it is the most popular SEO plug-in after Yoast SEO. The All in One SEO Pack is an alternative to Yoast SEO and only one WordPress SEO plug-in is required for a website.

SEO Press is a very powerful SEO plug-in and it includes all the necessary features of a SEO plug-in like Meta title, description, image, XML sitemaps, and redirects. Excellent features and ease of use characterise a typical SEO Press plug-in for WordPress Content Management System. The premium version of SEO Press is cheaper when compared to other prominent SEO plug-ins available in the market. Rank Math is a user friendly SEO plug-in and it is used for optimizing website for search engines and social media. Keywordtool.io is the best free keyword tool available today and it shows keyword suggestions from Google, Bing, Yahoo, Amazon and Fiverr.

The keywordtool.io can be used to generate keyword ideas by typing in a keyword and keyword suggestions in keywordtool.io are gathered from the auto suggest feature of Google. WordPress is well known for being SEO friendly and WordPress plug-ins will make a website SEO powerhouse. The Yoast SEO WordPress plug-in focuses on creating better content and optimizing the website. Page analysis tool, technical WordPress search engine optimization, and XML sitemaps functionality are the prime features of Yoast SEO. Yoast SEO continues its invincible journey of excellence through the corridors of web marketing.

The Yoast SEO can quickly scan any page for images and it checks whether the Meta description is up to par. All in One SEO Pack has been offering an easy to use solution for search engine optimization challenges ever since its inception. XML sitemap, Google Analytics support, automatic optimization of titles, and automatic generation of Meta tags are the colourful features of All in One SEO. All in one WP Security and Firewall and WP Touch Mobile plug-in are other prominent search engine optimization plug-ins for WordPress. Yoast SEO can be used to create XML sitemap, verify site in Web Master Tools, create title, and create Meta description.

Web masters can set custom title tags, Meta descriptions, and Meta robot tags using the Yoast SEO plug-in. All in one SEO pack has obvious similarities with Yoast SEO and it is highly customizable. The All in one SEO pack can be used to block bad bots, add site links search box markup, and auto generate Meta descriptions. Rank Math is a powerful SEO plug-in and user friendliness is the striking feature of Rank Math. It is packed with features like Google Search Console integration, redirection, rich snippets markup and card previews for Facebook.

The SEO Framework is a SEO plug-in which works as an excellent alternative to Yoast and All in One SEO Pack. Improving WordPress SEO is crucial for increasing traffic to a website and it paves the way towards organic traffic. Lots of individuals choose WordPress to start blogging since it is SEO friendly and WordPress ensures that the code it generates follows the latest SEO practices. SEO friendly URL structure should be used in WordPress and some of the best WordPress SEO practices include properly using categories, doing internal linking, and using HTTPS. WordPress is a best content management system from SEO viewpoint and it is a well optimized content management system.

Best Search Engine Optimization Software

The list of most prominent best search engine optimization software includes SEO Panel, SEM Rush, Ahrefs, Moz Pro, SE Ranking, SpyFu, Advance Web Ranking, and Serp Stat. SEO Panel is an award winning open source SEO software and it has heralded change in the web marketing industry. It is a SEO control panel for multiple websites equipped with features like automatic directory submission tool, keyword position checker, web master tools, social media checker and sitemap generator. The core features of SEO Panel include A/B testing, content management, keyword research, link management, multilingual support and user management. SEM Rush is an all in one marketing SEO tool and it is used by millions of professionals all over the globe.

The SEM Rush is generally used to fix technical website issues, improve the health of back link profile and track local rankings. It ensures a smooth flow between the team members and saves time on routine web marketing tasks. Ahrefs is a web marketing tool trusted by thousands of SEO professionals and it is one of the most prominent SEO software. Moz Pro is an All in One suite of SEO Tools and it is the best in-class SEO software of the contemporary age. It features tools for local Search Engine Optimization and enterprise Search Engine Results Page analytics.

SE Ranking is cloud based SEO software and it is a very powerful SEO tool for monitoring SEO optimization results. SpyFu is a competitive keyword research tool for Google Ads, Pay per Click and Search Engine Optimization. Advanced Web Ranking is SEO tool recommended for digital agencies and in-house SEO teams. The Advanced Web Ranking has streamlined innovation in the web marketing arena and it has been used by more than 18000 companies worldwide. This top rated search engine optimization software supports Windows, Mac, Android, and iPhone.

Serp Stat is an all in one SEO platform for professionals and its key features include auditing, Google Analytics integration, keyword tracking, rank tracking, link management and competitor analysis. Wix features the best SEO for a website and Hub Spot Marketing Hub is prominent search engine optimization software. Some of the premium SEO software includes KW Finder, Deep Crawl, Majestic, AWR Cloud and Moz Pro. Comprehensive selection of keyword search, attractive pricing, simple user experience, interactive reporting, back link tracking, and ongoing site monitoring are the remarkable specialties of SpyFu. SpyFu is a smooth SEO optimization tool geared towards web marketing, sales and digital advertising professionals. SEM Rush is a comprehensive keyword research tool with features like back link tracking, project based SEO campaign structure, and keyword suggestions.

SEM Rush is often referred as the perfect SEO tool and SEO experts say that Moz Pro is really a SEO powerhouse. Moz Pro offers vast number of SEO tools for keyword research, position monitoring, and crawling. Great keyword research capability, advance SEO capabilities and low price punctuate the KW Finder SEO software. AWR Cloud is user friendly SEO software and search rank tracking is the coveted feature of AWR Cloud. The information available from the web marketing industry indicates that small and medium businesses are the key beneficiaries of AWR Cloud.

Exceptional crawling capability, keyword research, improved keyword suggestions, and domain monitoring are the glowing features of Ahrefs. Ahrefs is a fantastic Search Engine Optimization tool with top notch web crawling capabilities and back link indexing. Majestic is equipped with features like deep crawling, solid reporting, campaign functionality and Buzz Sumo integration. Some of the best free SEO tools are Bing Webmaster Tools, Data Studio, Enhanced Google Analytics Annotations, Google Analytics, Google Search Console, Keyword Hero and Moz Cast. Beam Us Up, Link Redirect Trace, Redirect Path, Screaming Frog, and Xenu are some of the SEO tools which are absolutely free. The Bing Webmaster Tools provide a full suite of website as well as search analytics and its keyword reports are very useful.

Google Keyword Planner is a tested tool for search engine optimization and SE Nuke and Magic Submitter are two prominent search engine optimization software. Ahrefs is highly useful in keyword research, competitor analysis, back link research, content research and web page rank tracking. SEO Spider is a free SEO tool used to crawl URLs and it collects data relating to images, links and codes of the website. Moz Pro is a powerful keyword research and planning tool for content creators and Raven Tools is SEO audit tool. Every SEO tool is helpful in boosting organic traffic and they are used for keyword research, link building, traffic analysis and competitor analysis.

SEM Rush, Google Keyword Planner, Uber Suggest, and Keyword.io are the best SEO tools for keyword research. The SEM Rush can be used to track paid traffic, social media driven traffic, desktop traffic and mobile traffic. SEM Rush is a popular keyword research tool and it is helpful in building a keyword strategy for SEO agencies. Google Ads account is required to access the features of Google Keyword Planner and it is equipped with the capabilities of discovering keywords and looking at keyword metrics. Uber Suggest is a free keyword tool and it will tell keyword volume, average cost per click, and related long tail keywords.

Keyword research is the backbone of search engine optimization and it has been an essential part of search engine optimization. Buzz Stream is an All in One SEO package featuring domain research, email marketing, and project management. The Buzz Stream provides information on overall rankings, related social media accounts, authority and domain age. MoZ Pro is a suite of SEO tools and it has some similarities with SEM Rush, the innovative SEO software.

Key Functions of Moz Pro

Research how competitive a keyword is

Get suggestions on related keywords

Investigate competitors

Use a Chrome extension to look into other domains

Compare multiple keywords

Linkody is the easiest way to track link building campaigns and it can be used to analyze the back links of a website. Woo rank is almost similar to Hubspot's website grader and it provides tips to improve the usability of the website. The Woo Rank analyzes overall status of the website including SEO, usability, performance, and back links. The price of Woo Rank premium version starts at $50 per month and the Varvy SEO tool tells whether a site follows all Google SEO guidelines. It checks for things like page speed issues, mobile friendliness, and on page Search Engine Optimization.

Blog Search Engine Optimization

Search engine optimization is a key component of blog marketing and SEO friendly blog design is an important thing as far as blog search engine optimization is concerned. Every blog post should be optimized for SEO and great title is an inseparable element of blogging SEO. Targeting the right keywords, focusing on low difficulty keywords, focusing on long tail keywords, using keywords in the title and writing compelling titles are few blog search engine optimization tips. Making the blog responsive is absolutely important and it is ideal to pick a responsive WordPress theme. A blog should be optimized for featured snippets and the images in blog should be optimized for increased web traffic.

Blogging really helps search engine optimization and blog is a practical tool to add more content to a website. A blog keeps people on website for longer and long form posts perform better than short form posts. Blogging is helpful in targeting long tail keywords and long tail keywords are essential for SEO strategy. Blog gives more opportunities for internal linking and SEO is all about links as well as internal links. A quality blog gives reasons to link back to the website and blogs are helpful in connecting with an audience.

Blogging SEO should essentially focus on long term keywords and it is essential to do SERP research for every blog topic. Blogs should be optimized for rich content and the images in a blog should be optimized for search engines. Every blog post should have at least one image and it is a recommended practice to add alt text, image file name and caption text. Guest posting on relevant blogs is another key blogging search engine optimization strategy and creating valuable content is the first and foremost part of blogging SEO. Internal links can be added to a typical blog post and old blog posts should be updated to keep them current.

Influencers can be featured in a typical blog post and images, videos, Infographics and podcasts should be used in an ideal blog post. Blogging is the best thing to improve search engine optimization and creating regular content which is always good is the key part of blogging SEO. Writing SEO friendly blog post is an art and a blog post should be equipped with headings and sub headings. People will link, share and tweet a high quality blog post which will increase search engine optimization rankings. Ideal blog posts should be readable and SEO friendly and it is ideal to create copy that visitors like.

Bloggers should do keyword research before starting blog posting and the best blog post should be a good piece of writing. According to successful bloggers, every blog post should have introduction, body and conclusion. There should be logical reason for starting a new paragraph in blogs and each paragraph should have unique idea or subject. Headings in a blog post are important for search engine optimization and keywords should be used in the sub headings of a blog post. It is a well known fact that Google likes long articles and an ideal blog post should be kept to 2500 words.

Linking to previous content on the blog is a well known search engine optimization practice and link structure is important for Google rank. Posting high quality, well written, engaging, informative and keyword rich articles in blog is the most important SEO tip. The Yoast SEO plug-in can be used to write user friendly, engaging, well written and readable blog posts. SEO blog tips pave the way towards increased organic traffic and a sitemap should be built before starting the process of blog writing. Bloggers should necessarily focus on the blog headline and the keyword should be included in the blog title.

According to SEO masterminds, keywords should be used generously in heading 2 and heading 3 of a typical long form blog post. The primary keyword should be closely related to the blog post and the ideal primary keyword should be popular with users. It is ideal to select keywords with a low competition rate and the blog content should be written for real readers, not for search engines. SEO bloggers should keep their readers always in mind and writing a blog post below 300 words is not at all recommended. The primary keyword should be naturally used throughout the text and the ideal blog post should have a keyword density of three percent.

The secondary keywords should be used once throughout the text and secondary keywords provide additional context for content. The primary keyword should be used in the first paragraph and the primary keyword should be used in sub heading too. The sub heading in a paragraph should be formatted with H2, H3, and H4 and great SEO content uses sub headings. The keyword should be used towards the end of the page and writing original content is a vital SEO step. Writing original content can be used to boost the SEO power of a website and it is important to write grammatically correct content in blog posts without any spelling mistake.

The best blog posts are written for easy consumption and both search engines and readers will value high quality content. According to blogging experts, lengthy and complex terms should not be used in a blog post and it is ideal to use short sentences. Both inbound and outbound links can be added in a blog post for better visibility and hyperlinks help search engines understand pages. The primary keyword should be used in the page title and it should also be used in the permalink. The SEO title of a blog post should include primary keyword and it should not exceed fifty five characters.

Using the primary keyword in the Meta description is an excellent SEO blogging tip and the SEO Meta description adds backend information. The Meta description of a blog post should not exceed 155 characters and using the primary keyword in image ALT tag is a SEO blogging tip. Adding images to a blog post makes it look authentic and things like title of the post, blog structure, formatting, headings and paragraphs are important in blogging SEO. It is to be kept in mind that Search Engine Optimization friendly blog post is a user friendly blog post. The finest meaning of search engine optimization is to publish the content that both search engines and users can understand.

Career in Search Engine Optimization

Search engine optimization features a star studded career and it is a lucrative career opportunity in the contemporary world. Very few persons study search engine optimization in the university and SEO career is popular among Information Technology professionals. Search engine optimization has created huge influx of jobs all over the world and SEO professional is a careerist specialized in search engine algorithms. Search engine optimization is taught as a part of web marketing today and most of the SEO professionals master the subject through short term courses and certifications. A typical search engine optimization specialist will be skilled in content writing, web marketing, HTML, link building, competitor analysis, and keyword research.

Search engine optimization professional will be skilled in using tools like Moz, Google Keyword Planner, SE Nuke and Magic Submitter. SEO experts are in high demand all over the world especially in countries like United States of America, United Kingdom, Singapore, India and Germany. Content marketer and web developer are the glowing careers in search engine optimization field. Career in search engine optimization offers tremendous growth opportunities and SEO career is really exciting. Search engine optimization skills are a gateway to number of careers including search engine marketer, business marketing consultant, digital marketer, marketing analyst and content marketer.

The job responsibilities of search engine marketer include pay per click marketing, advertising, and managing customer relationships. A typical business marketing consultant will be well versed in client based consultancy, planning marketing initiatives and public relation management. Content marketer will be an expert in creating web content, designing blogs, designing videos and executing marketing plan. Search Engine Marketing requires skills like pay per click, advertising and customer relationship management. Some of the SEM professionals specialize in paid search and search engine marketing specialist will be a master expert in Google Ads and Bing Ads.

Some search engine optimization professionals are public speakers, professional business consultants and internet marketing consultants. Search engine optimization professional plays a pivotal role in improving the marketing and strategic planning of a company. Digital marketers take care of search engine optimization, search engine marketing, social media marketing, and pay per click. A web marketer will have relevant qualifications in web marketing, communications and strategic marketing. The key job responsibilities of a web marketing analyst are tracking the performance of marketing initiatives and identifying opportunities for new marketing initiatives. Content marketers are equipped with solid Search Engine Optimization skills and content marketing professionals are key members of the marketing team.

Search engine optimization requires a team of web marketers, SEO specialists, content strategists, and technology experts. Larger companies will probably have large search engine optimization teams and the job responsibilities of SEO managers vary depending on the company. Starting a business in SEO or web marketing is an innovative idea and it will provide rich dividends. The need for well trained SEO professionals is growing on a day by day basis and the most common job titles in SEO are digital marketing manager, web marketing specialist, SEO specialist, web developer, web marketing analyst, content strategist and SEO manager. SEO is something more than a successful career and it requires combination of skills to become a rock star SEO professional.

Search engine optimization has become a hot career opportunity in developed countries of the world. Individuals passionate about web marketing, websites, writing and blogging can enter the shining professional landscape of SEO. Logic, patience, dedication, hard work and common sense are the ideal traits of SEO professional. Search Engine Optimization will remain a very popular career option in the near future too thanks to the explosive growth of search engines. There will be more demand for SEO professionals in the United States of America in the coming years.

Many graduates and web designers all over the world are switching on their career to search engine optimization. A SEO professional should always update his knowledge about web marketing since SEO is constantly evolving. Many SEO professionals start their career as SEO executives in web marketing companies and there are lots of rewarding opportunities for freelance SEO professionals. A typical SEO professional will have encyclopaedic knowledge of Google Ads and Google Analytics. Many of the SEO professionals are Google certified professionals and the most common designations in SEO career are junior SEO executive, senior SEO executive, SEO analyst, link building expert, SEO project manager and Google Ads Specialist.

SEO professional wears many hats like blogger, content writer, web marketer, affiliate marketer and freelance SEO consultant. Search engine optimization is unquestionably an excellent career choice and being a good writer is an extremely valuable skill possessed by SEO professional. SEO has become a definitive career choice and it is an attractive career option festooned with immense career growth. SEO professionals should keep in mind that SEO is both an art and science and this philosophy gets reflected in SEO career too. There is always something new to learn in search engine optimization and it is the best career for innovative minds.

SEO is a career field with lots of amazingly intelligent people and fabled web marketing professionals. Search engine optimization is a career field which is extremely competitive and SEO professionals should be agile and creative in order to succeed in their careers. Search Engine Optimization is the field of smart, passionate, and tech savvy individuals who are out of the box thinkers. SEO is a career of lifelong learning and SEO career of today encompasses content marketing, keyword research, technical SEO and local SEO. Search engine optimization careers have been around for the past two decades and career in SEO needs analytical, communication and development skills.

SEO experts will have a crystal clear knowledge of on page SEO, off page SEO and technical SEO. He will have comprehensive understanding of different SEO terminologies like keyword, keyword research, link building, back links, white hat SEO, and black hat SEO. SEO expert will have to optimize the page title, Meta description, headings and content of a page. The writing skills of SEO professional should be top notch and SEO professionals are equipped with basic web development skills. SEO specialist needs to know HTML, WordPress, JavaScript, website structure, Microsoft Excel and Google Docs.

Content Marketing and Search Engine Optimization

Content marketing is unquestionably the best way to improve search engine optimization and both search engine optimization and content marketing are two essential tools in the arsenal of an internet marketer. The content marketing strategies will take the branding efforts of a business organization into the next level. Integrated content marketing strategy is an inseparable component of search engine optimization. Combination of content marketing and search engine optimization provide amazing web marketing results. Developing SEO content strategy ensures that content marketing and search engine optimization work hand in hand.

The combination of content marketing and search engine optimization are beneficial for online businesses. Content is a key factor in search engine optimization and keyword research is the most important part of content marketing. Content marketing is a web marketing strategy which focuses on creating relevant and valuable content. The content marketing is not always focused on selling and the leading benefits of content marketing are brand awareness, competitive advantage, media visibility, website traffic, leads as well as conversions. Content marketing can benefit small businesses in innumerable ways and the second part of content marketing involves promoting content in different channels like social media vehicles. According to ace web marketers, the final goal of content marketing is to build relationships with leads and customers.

It is quite important to create content that appeals to visitors and content marketing is a very powerful web marketing channel. According to rock star web marketing professionals, relevant content creation is the most effective SEO tactic. Businesses can improve the visibility on search engines by creating content focused around targeted keywords. Search engine optimization and content marketing work together to reach new leads through search engines like Google. SEO affects the effectiveness of content marketing and content marketing strategy should be developed only after researching the target market.

Video content, ebooks and white papers are the most popular types of content marketing in the contemporary age. Well written content is an essential component of content marketing and the content in a website should be updated to remain effective. Web marketers should understand that search engine optimization and content marketing are two different tools. Developing an effective content strategy ensures that SEO and content marketing bring amazing results. An effective combination of Search Engine Optimization and content marketing boost online business success. Both search engine optimization and content marketing have changed the web marketing world in unimaginable ways. Search engine optimization without content marketing is like a body without a soul and SEO is strategized around content marketing.

Fresh, unique, creative, informative, trustworthy and authentic content is the key component of content marketing. Content marketing is only successful if it is equipped with appropriate SEO and SEO plus content marketing has huge potential. SEO is actually all about content marketing and the combination of SEO and content marketing features wondrous web marketing achievements. SEO and content marketing work well together and both of them are differentiated from one another. Success of content marketing can be ensured by applying SEO techniques in its implementation.

The well known adage 'content is king' illustrates the importance of content marketing and search engine optimization. High quality content earns so many back links and it is essential to optimize content with relevant keywords. It is a well known fact that SEO and content marketing are the top rated web marketing tools of today. Both SEO and content marketing have undergone huge transformation ever since the inception of Google. Content marketing is a consistent approach to retain a specific audience and it leads to increase in conversions. SEO and content marketing are interrelated concepts and search engine optimization is more technical than content marketing. Content marketing has a wider scope than search engine optimization and it focuses on satisfying the needs of human audiences.

It would be a huge mistake to consider content marketing and search engine optimization as two separate entities. Content marketing is necessary for getting higher search engine rankings and it is the practical application of SEO. The content marketing is undoubtedly the best way to attract inbound links from readers and both SEO and content marketing are closely interrelated. Content marketing focuses on retaining users for a lifetime and the content should create awareness about the product. Businesses of today need to focus on integrating content marketing with search engine optimization.

Content marketing can fulfil the varied needs of search engine optimization and social media channels can be used to distribute content effectively. Proper content marketing strategy is an inseparable element of search engine optimization of today. Keyword research, keyword optimization, content organization and content promotion are key steps involved in content marketing. Product pages and blog posts are two most prominent types of search engine optimization content. A good product page will serve as both Search Engine Optimization content and Pay per Click landing page. A blog is the best way to create regular stream of SEO content and blog posts are generally more engaging. Blog posts attract link from product pages and articles, listicles and guides are other popular forms of content marketing.

Videos are considered as a great way to attract target audience and they help a website to get ranked in search engines very easily. Video tutorials of products are another popular form of content marketing which take the internet by storm. Infographics, slide shows, directories and glossaries are other forms of popular content marketing. Content marketing is the best way to improve search engine rankings and overall search engine optimization. It is a well known fact that content marketing is a subset of inbound marketing and Google favours the elements of a good content marketing plan.

Content creation is an essential part of solid search engine optimization strategy and content marketing gives businesses a competitive advantage in search engine rankings. Google prefers substantial content and internet marketing maestros say that long form content is always the best. Unique content helps a website to get better search engine rankings and the benefits of content marketing go beyond search engine marketing. Content marketing fills gaps in the sales funnel and it exposes businesses to additional audiences. Content in a website should be developed keeping target audience in mind and the approach of internet marketers towards content marketing and SEO are slightly different.

Google Search Engine Optimization

Keyword research and on page optimization are two key elements of Google search engine optimization. Valuable keywords should be placed in body of the text, title, Meta title as well as sub headings. Sub headings and H2 headings are invaluable spots for Google search engine optimization. Keywords should be incorporated into the Meta title, Meta description, image file name as well as attribute. Google SEO involves making changes to website design as well as content and creating engaging SEO focused content is the key aspect of Google search engine optimization.

Both on page and off page factors influence Google search engine optimization and overall content relevance, keywords in body, keywords in description, keyword in title and keyword in H1 are the key Google ranking factors. High quality content is the most vital component of Google search engine optimization and blog posts, articles, social media content, ebooks, whitepapers, Infographics, and video tutorials are the key types of content valued by Google. Fresh content is the principal element of Google SEO and Google loves quality, well written content. Title tag, Meta description, sub headings, internal links, and image name are few on page Google SEO ranking factors. The title tag should be seventy characters or less and the Meta description should include keyword.

Google will penalize websites who use keywords too many times and the content in a website should be specific. Website design is a key element of on page Google search engine optimization and Google likes mobile friendly websites. Organic SEO is a process of optimizing website copy and HTML in order to help a website rank higher on search engines like Google. It has been pointed out that Google organic search engine optimization takes time, patience, perseverance and consistency. Understanding localized keyword research is an integral part of Google search engine optimization.

Implementing the keywords in on-site copy is an excellent Google search engine optimization strategy. Google search engine optimization is a fast paced and dynamic world which is more complex than ever today. According to prominent web marketers, Google SEO is about great user experience and generating new leads as well as revenue. Google search engine optimization is not about magic tricks and organic search is one of the most profitable marketing channels. Creating good content is the most important Google search engine optimization strategy and properly executed content marketing is a goldmine for Google SEO. The search engine tycoon Google focuses on useful content today and adding quality content consistently is a vital Google SEO strategy.

Creating a mobile friendly website is an integral part of Google search engine optimization strategy. Indexing and crawling are two important aspects of Google Search Engine Optimization. Using HTTPS, creating simple page URLs, and preventing duplicate URLs are Google search engine optimization tips. One of the biggest components of search engine optimization for Google is keyword research. Some of the best keyword tools for Google search engine optimization are Keywordtool.io, Uber Suggest, and Google Trends.

It is quite important to create a compelling, unique and descriptive title as a part of Google SEO strategy. Internet marketers can give Meta description more power with summarizing the content, limiting Meta description to 155 characters, and creating a unique description. The bulk of Google Search Engine Optimization focuses on content and Google's preferred content includes lots of mediums like video. Creating keyword optimized content is a key Google Search Engine Optimization strategy and checking the readability of content is a useful SEO tip. Image optimization is valuable from the perspective of Google and images should be properly optimized for Google. The image file name should be short and creating image alt text is an excellent Google SEO tip. Only standard image formats like JPEG, PNG, GIF, and BMP should be used in a website and it helps in Google SEO.

Google Search Engine Optimization is an essential part of the website strategy of every company and making the website faster is a prominent Google SEO tip. The search engine giant Google uses site speed as a ranking factor and site speed is important for search engines. Reviewing page elements, enabling browser caching, and reducing plug-ins are three essential Google SEO tips. HTTPS has some SEO benefits too and Google brands HTTP sites as non secure websites today. Google has introduced HTTPS as a ranking factor in Google search algorithm and optimizing the mobile version of the website is another Google SEO tip.

Mobile responsive sites will get indexed well in search engine rankings and Google's mobile friendly test tool can be used to find out whether the website is mobile responsive. Google rewards websites with strong user engagement and using high quality images throughout the content is an excellent Google SEO tip. Internet marketers should focus on the user experience of website as a Google search engine optimization strategy. User experience is an important part of Google Search Engine Optimization and Google favours websites with a positive user experience. Creating engaging and valuable content is the best part of Google Search Engine Optimization.

It has been reported that Google SEO is the elegant mixture of content marketing and search engine optimization. Content marketing plays a key role in improving search engine rankings and creating engaging content is the first Google SEO tip. Google, the creative brainchild of Larry Page and Sergey Brin rewards original, fresh and quality content. Content is still king as far as Google SEO is concerned and Google takes into account how fresh the content in a website is. Google rewards sites that provide new content on constant basis and strengthening social media presence is a Google SEO tip.

Sharing quality content on social media pages is another vital SEO trick since users are searching for topics on Facebook, YouTube, Instagram and Twitter. Using long tail keywords is a best Search Engine Optimization strategy and it is one of the fundamental Google SEO tricks. Long tail keywords will bring specific traffic and qualified leads to a website and the site content should be optimized for Google featured snippets. Creating optimized online video content will help a website to get better search engine rankings in Google. Search engines including the Google loves video content and YouTube video marketing is another Google SEO tip.

How to Do Search Engine Optimization?

Keyword research is an integral component of search engine optimization and Google Keyword Planner is the keyword research tool recommended for beginner SEO technocrats. SEM Rush and Word Tracker are two other prominent SEO keyword research tools popular today. Designing a mobile friendly website is a basic SEO requirement and Google ranks organic search results from desktop and mobile devices. Publishing fresh content regularly is a top rated search engine optimization tactic and link authority is a major component of search engine optimization. Understanding of Google Analytics is essential to measure the impact of search engine optimization.

Search engine optimization requires a long term commitment since search algorithms change very frequently. It will take months to see the actual results of search engine optimization and building a great website is the first and foremost step of search engine optimization. Including a sitemap is a best search engine optimization practice and making SEO friendly URLs is very important. Google Ads give information about the actual search volume for the keywords and unique title and Meta description should be used in every page. Creating great and unique content is the basic principle of search engine optimization of the contemporary age. The creation of unique content is a challenge for online retailers and great content is the best way to get inbound links.

Keywords should be used as an anchor text when linking internally and building links from trusted directories like Yahoo and DMOZ is a best SEO practice. Creating great content on consistent basis is the most common strategy for search engine optimization. Distributing press releases online is an effective SEO tactic and search engines especially Google loves blogs. Using social media marketing wisely is a top rated search engine optimization strategy popular today. Internet marketers should take advantage of local search engines and tools like Google Webmaster Central, Bing Webmaster tools and Yahoo Site Explorer.

Diversifying the traffic sources is an essential search engine optimization strategy and blogging is a great way to build an audience of loyal prospects. Choosing the right URL, creating titles for each page, utilizing anchor text, adding alt text to images, and giving site structure right headers are basic SEO strategies. SEO is not very hard like many of the web marketers think and a web marketer should have a clear idea of how Google works. Internet marketers should keep in mind that Google is getting smarter as days pass by and Google has become faster at shutting down spammy sites. Business owners and web marketers can reap the rich benefits of search engine optimization.

SEO is a set of tactics focused on improving the visibility of a website in search engines like Google, Yahoo and Bing. Search engine optimization is an ongoing process and SEO is a marketing strategy which attracts qualified traffic. SEO is helpful in achieving a high click through rate and keywords and back links play a vital role in SEO ranking. The key SEO ranking factors are direct website visits, bounce rate, total referring domains, total back links, content length, website security, keyword in anchor, keyword density, and video in page. SEO is essential to every website and lead generation is the ultimate objective of search engine optimization.

Search engine optimization is focused on attracting visitors that are actively searching for information. The list of white hat SEO strategies include relevant content, well labelled images, relevant page titles, and standards compliant HTML. On page SEO deals with title tag, Meta tags, Meta descriptions, Meta keywords, keywords in text, keywords in H1, H2, H3 tags, hyperlinks and image descriptions. Off page SEO deals with social media links, Google reviews, and reviews from sites like LinkedIn. Attracting people interested in content is the crux of search engine optimization and the Google Ads is aimed at advertisers.

A website should be structured for ease of use and site directory of a website should be organized properly. The content in a website should be checked for grammar, spelling, syntax and readability for better SEO. It has been pointed out that search engine optimization involves creative and technical activities. SEO ensures that a website is technically sound, accessible, and offers an excellent user experience. Building strong site architecture and providing clear navigation are two essential SEO tactics.

It is a fact that Google is increasingly paying attention to user experience and there are many SEO benefits of using the perfect user experience. Responsive design and mobile optimization have become key parts of search engine optimization of today. Internal linking provides the audience with further reading options and it helps in crawling and indexing site. A link from authority website is considered as very valuable and publishing evergreen content is a vital SEO strategy. Registering with 'Google My Business' is very helpful local search engine optimization tip and Google Trends, Browseo, Screaming Frog, GT Metrix, and Rank Checker are the free SEO tools available to boost search engine rankings. Google Trends is the perfect keyword tool and Browseo shows how a search engine views a website.

Search Engine Optimization is one of the most effective ways to build traffic to a website and the selection of right hosting provider is a vital factor for SEO. The WordPress specific hosting plan should be reliable and it should have a reputation for excellent performance. It is necessary to select a WordPress theme optimized for search engines and the theme plays a key role in SEO. WordPress themes are specifically designed to improve search engine optimization and it is ideal to use dedicated SEO plug-ins like Yoast SEO. Creating site maps, using heading tags throughout content, building content around keywords, incorporating useful links, and using responsive design are other key SEO tips.

Google uses responsive design as a ranking factor and it is recommended to choose a WordPress theme that supports responsive design. Image optimization has a great impact on SEO and each image in a typical website should be properly optimized. Longer content gets indexed well in search engines and it will increase perceived credibility along with providing value to readers. Internet marketers should focus on quality content since it is the most important ranking factor in Google. The basics of on page website optimization include making the website structure clear, including primary keyword in page URL, using hyphens instead of underscore in URLs, and choosing a static URL address.

Joomla Search Engine Optimization

Joomla search engine optimization paves the way towards increased search traffic and gaining organic users. Page loading and site speed are key components of Joomla search engine optimization. Using Joomla SEO plug-ins is a great idea and enabling search friendly URL is another Joomla search engine optimization tip. Creating quality content is the vital aspect of Joomla SEO and Joomla search engine optimization is not that something limited to Meta title and description. Joomla SEO is the practice of optimizing a Joomla website for boosting conversion and ranking.

On page SEO is really important for Joomla website and title tag is one of the most important Joomla SEO ranking factors. The standard page title length in a Joomla website should be up to 65-70 characters and it is ideal to limit keyword density in a Joomla web page to 2%. Image ALT tag optimization is very important in Joomla search engine optimization and the image ALT tags tell search engine bots what the image is about. Content below 500 words will not provide any SEO benefits in Joomla and internal links should be used 2-3 times in every Joomla page. Joomla on page search engine optimization is a combination of different factors and Joomla SEO is not something which can be achieved overnight.

Enabling search engine friendly URLs is the preliminary step of Joomla search engine optimization. Being URL friendly is considered as a ranking factor by prominent search engines and paying more attention to long tail keyword is a top rated Joomla SEO practice. Permalinks are incredibly important in Joomla search engine optimization and it is quite important to use descriptive page titles in Joomla. Images have SEO power in Joomla search engine optimization and setting up a sitemap is a Joomla SEO strategy. It is relatively easy to add a sitemap to Joomla and Joomla search engine sitemap is formatted specially to the specifications of search engines.

The list of perfect Joomla SEO extensions includes Aimy sitemap, OS Map, JSiteMap, and Qlue sitemap. The Joomla site should look good on mobile and some of the best third party Joomla components for SEO include Sh404 Sef and Artio JoomSEF. Title is a critical factor for Joomla SEO rankings and SEO Joomla extensions can be used to create title tag. Page meta description is absolutely important in Joomla search engine optimization and creating valuable content is another key factor in Joomla SEO just like WordPress SEO. Keywords should be used in the Joomla page title and the keyword placement in page title plays a key role in Joomla SEO.

Local Search Engine Optimization

Both big and small business organizations can attract more customers using local search engine optimization. Local search engine optimization will help a company to get remarkable online visibility and local SEO is closely interrelated with link building, 'Google My Business', reviews, local rankings, business listings, and onsite optimization. Local search engine optimization is also referred as local search engine marketing and it is a highly effective way to market business online. Businesses can promote their products and services to local customers using the infinite potential of local search engine optimization. Local SEO is entirely different from standard SEO and it is worth investing in local search engine optimization.

'Google My Business Profile' is a critical aspect of local search engine optimization and it feeds info to variety of places. 'Google My Business' listing includes lots of information like offer, contact details, business descriptions, and category. Making the 'Google My Business' profile up to date and accurate is the first step of local search engine optimization. The 'Google My Business' is an incredibly powerful marketing medium and getting citations for local business is a standard local search engine optimization strategy. The three principal elements of local search ranking are proximity, relevance as well as prominence.

It is a fact that local search engine optimization changes constantly and SEO agencies invest heavily in local SEO. Local SEO has become the sanctum sanctorum of local businesses and website localization, citation building, managing reviews and getting quality back links are vital local SEO strategies. Localizing the website refers to including city, country, or region name naturally throughout the website. Bing Places for Business is the Microsoft equivalent to 'Google My Business' and Yelp is another prominent local business directory. The authority of online reviews, overall quality of reviews, and authority of review sites are important factors for local SEO rankings.

Naturally obtaining back links from high quality websites is a top local search engine optimization tactic. Links from newspapers, news sites and bloggers will be helpful in improving search visibility in online platforms. Local SEO services will help typical businesses to attract new customers and local customers are turning to the internet to find local businesses. The local search engine optimization is highly targeted and people perform local searches to find a local business. Local SEO has the highest conversion rate and local directories dominate the first page of local search results. Local directory marketing is a local search engine optimization strategy and it has higher conversion rate.

City Search and Four Square are well known local business directories of today and the local SEO covers both PC and mobile internet access. Local SEO is a great return on investment and it is efficient and cost effective as a marketing strategy. Getting listed on 'Google My Business' will help a business get ranked well in search engine results pages. Local businesses can immensely get benefitted from web marketing and many of the best local SEO opportunities are free. It is free to claim listing on Google My Business, Bing Places for Business and numerous leading local business directories.

Local search engine optimization can be used to increase the online reputation of a company and it attracts hundreds of new customers. Businesses implement different SEO strategies to attract more customers and a business can be grown by leaps and bounds using local SEO. Local SEO strategies will become stronger and stronger in the upcoming days of massive internet explosion. Local search engine optimization is beneficial to local businesses, plumbers, artisans, accountants and florists. Small businesses can make more money through local search engine optimization and optimizing the 'Google My Business' listing is the key aspect of local Search Engine Optimization.

Local SEO is something more than 'Google My Business' listing and people search for local businesses using search engines like Bing, Yelp and Apple Maps. Most internet users use Google for searching local businesses and title and Meta description tags matter in local SEO just like standard SEO. Writing titles and descriptions is considered as an art in local Search Engine Optimization world. It is important to get the business name, address and phone number of a business listed in local directories. The 'Google My Business' offers incredible opportunities for local businesses like coffee shops, restaurants, bakeries and workshops.

'Google My Business' listing should be optimized with description, categories, business hours and types of payments accepted. Small businesses should upload the logo and photos of business in 'Google My Business' listing. The process of registering in Bing Places for Business is almost similar to 'Google My Business' listing. It is mandatory to verify the physical address of business in order to get registered in both 'Google My Business' and Bing Places for Business. Online reviews are an integral component of local search engine optimization and the online reviews are often treated as a personal recommendation. Tools like Reputation Loop, Get Five Stars, and Trust Pilot can be used to track and manage online reviews.

Local search engine optimization is a branch of SEO which deals with optimizing a website to be found in local search results. Local SEO is known as a strategic process that focuses on optimization efforts of local brick and mortar businesses. Content optimization, on page optimization, and link building are parts of local search engine optimization. Local search is quite important for brick and mortar businesses as well as mom and pop stores in the contemporary age of Google. Lawyers, law firms, doctors, and restaurants can get benefitted from local search engine optimization.

Local SEO is all about optimizing for a better local audience and optimizing the city name and address details are integral components of local search engine optimization. Content optimization is the main tool of local search engine optimization and local pages are mainly added for SEO reasons. It is to be kept in mind that local SEO is not just about search engines and word of mouth and print brochure contribute to local SEO. Local SEO features number of factors that help businesses address local audience by better rankings in search engines. The most important ranking factors for local SEO are on page optimization, inbound links, Google My Business, external directory references, search personalization, and reviews.

According to the information available from ace web marketing experts, local search engine optimization relies on the quantity and quality of inbound links. Some of the best directories for local search include Yelp, Foursquare, Merchant Circle, and Internet Yellow Pages. User behavioural and mobile usage are key local search engine optimization ranking factors of today. Examples of user behavioural and mobile usage ranking factors include click through rates and check-ins. It has been said that the quantity and diversity of online reviews affect local search engine optimization.

Facebook likes and Twitter followers affect local search engine optimization results in Google, Bing as well as Yahoo. According to Google, local search engine rankings are mainly based on relevance and prominence. Adding complete and detailed business information is an essential local search engine optimization tip. Duplicate listings in local search directories, inconsistency with business name, incorrect categories used in local directories, and unverified listings in local directories will hamper local search engine optimization. Local SEO does not need to insert location throughout the content and adding address and phone number in the footer of website is a best local search engine optimization practice. Facebook is always good for local SEO and using a consistent format for address is important in local SEO.

The Google's list of local SEO ranking factors evolves constantly and Moz Local is a fantastic tool used for detecting all the listings associated with business. The business name, address and phone number need to be consistent for better local search engine optimization results. 'Google My Business Listing' is a great place to start local search engine optimization and brief business description should be included in 'Google My Business Listing'. High quality images should be included in the 'Google My Business' listing and reviews are of great importance in local search engine optimization. Reviews are a critical Google local search engine optimization ranking factor and they help businesses to tackle the most important components of conversion including ranking, click through rate and conversion rate optimization.

Creating content catered to the niche is a basic Google local search engine optimization strategy and the Google Ads Keyword Planner can be used to find local SEO keywords. Acquiring back links from partners is a great local search engine optimization tip and conducting local link building is a crucial component of local SEO. Earning links from websites with a high domain authority in the local area is another key local search engine optimization strategy. Utilizing the social media platforms like Facebook, Twitter, Linked In and YouTube will provide fruitful local SEO benefits. Local SEO is essential to small businesses just like national SEO and it relies on marketing brands and products to local leads.

Optimizing local SEO leads to more website traffic, leads, and conversions and businesses will be losing significant amount of traffic without local SEO. Getting glowing five star reviews from customers is a very vital local search engine optimization tip. Online reviews are treated as personal recommendations in the contemporary business world and local SEO should be optimized for local search. It is an excellent local search engine optimization practice to create content based on local news stories or events. Some of the key content strategies include writing blog posts around local news, creating videos about local news, and setting up location specific web pages.

Optimizing the website for mobile will be helpful in the local search engine optimization efforts and traffic from local searches is often lucrative. Some of the tips to optimize website for mobile include using bigger fonts and using intuitive user interface for great user experience. Google keyword planner can be used to filter keyword searches based on location and it can be used to find a list of locally relevant keywords. The location specific 'About Us' page should include store hours, name, address, phone number, individualized descriptions, testimonials and promotions. Taking advantage of online business directories like Map Quest is a local search engine optimization tip.

On Page Search Engine Optimization

On page search engine optimization is the practice of optimizing individual web pages in order to rank higher in search results. The on page SEO refers to both the content as well as site structure and the objective of on page SEO is to rank as high as possible in the search engine results. The factors in Google's algorithm can be divided into on page factors and off page factors and on page factors include textual content, visual content, and user friendliness of the site. Technical excellence, awesome content, and flawless user experience are the key pillars of on page SEO. The SEO friendly platform of WordPress takes care of the technical aspects of a website and the plug-in Yoast SEO ensures that technical aspects of on page SEO are covered.

Excellent content is an inseparable element of on page search engine optimization and Google loves quality content. The content in a typical website should be interesting and easy to read and a beautifully designed website is a key on page SEO factor. Structured website, permanent monitoring, excellent content, right keywords, white hat strategies, deep site analysis and quality links are the principal elements of on page search engine optimization. Optimizing the content is the most important on page search engine optimization ranking factor and a web page should be tailored around one family of keywords. An ideal web page should be optimized around one keyword and all the connected keywords.

A golden rule of on page search engine optimization is to use keyword variations in prominent locations. The URL address should describe what the page is about and the URL address suffix should be a short summary of the page. URL should essentially contain the target keyword and it should be clear, readable and accessible. There are no strict rules about writing great content and smart internet marketers play with headlines, bolded text, and ordered list of elements. The content in a website should be written for people, not for search engines and at least one image should be used in the content.

Writing short paragraphs is a best strategy as far as content is concerned and the super keyword should be used 2 to 3 times throughout the page. The variations and synonyms of the super keyword should be used few times in a web article and keyword stuffing should be avoided. On page search engine optimization is crucial to the success of SEO campaign and on page SEO looks at what the page is about. The on page SEO is also called as on site SEO and title tag is the biggest on page Search Engine Optimization factor. According to self styled internet marketing professionals, the heading should accurately reflect the page content.

Keywords should be put into the URL if possible and optimizing the page to load faster is a great on page search engine optimization tip. The content in a web page should be useful to the reader and it is the basic on page search engine optimization principle. On page Search Engine Optimization ensures that site can be read by potential customers and search engine robots. Search engines can easily index web pages with good on page search engine optimization and the Google search engine algorithms emphasize on optimizing the pages for user. Meta description, HTML code, title tags and alt tags are the foundation of on page search engine optimization.

Overall content quality, page performance and content structure are the key on page search engine optimization factors. Keyword optimization is an important aspect of on page SEO and the focus of keyword optimization has shifted towards long tail keywords. Keywords should be included in the Meta description so that they can be picked up by search engine crawlers. The Meta description should be kept to fewer than 300 characters to ensure that the entire description is shown in search results. Title tag is a great opportunity to include relevant keywords and boost the searchability of a web page.

Enabling SSL (Secure Sockets Layer) is crucial for increasing security and visibility in search engines. Google prefers SSL enabled sites and SSL ensures that the information entered on the website is very safe. An organized URL structure is one of the most important on page SEO elements and it makes navigation efficient for visitors. Offbeat internet marketing companies give special emphasis on URL structure and it is quite important to use easy to understand URLs. Internally linking related pages is another vital on page search engine optimization element and it keeps visitors engaged longer.

It is a very well known fact that major on page search engine optimization factors deal with content quality and structure. Internet marketers of today need to consider the image file size on pages, reduce redirects, improve the mobile responsiveness of sites and minimize the amount of CSS/JavaScript. The ultimate objective of on page SEO is to increase organic traffic and on page SEO deals exclusively with the strategic placement of keywords on the page. On page SEO is the fundamental aspect of search engine optimization and it helps search engines understand the website better. On page SEO is important if a business organization needs targeted visitors to knock on the online doorstep.

Choosing the right set of keywords is a principal component of on page search engine optimization. Keyword research is the first important step in any on page SEO campaign and the right set of keywords attract targeted audience to a website. Choosing good domain names is a vital element of on page search engine optimization and creating unique content that online readers want to share is a key on page SEO tactic. Unique and high quality content is the best component of on page search engine optimization strategies. The content in a web page should provide visitors a good user experience including graphics and navigational aids.

Videos, images and non text content in a website should be optimized for better on page search engine optimization results. Creating product specific landing page is another vital on page search engine optimization tip. It is an excellent search engine optimization practice to create as many landing pages as possible. Effective on page SEO techniques will boost search engine rankings and it is an inseparable element of running SEO campaign. The ultimate goal of on page SEO is to speak the search engine's language and on page SEO is important because it provides search engines with number of signals to understand what the content is about.

Off Page Search Engine Optimization

Off page search engine optimization refers to actions taken outside of the website to impact rankings within search engine result pages. Effective off page Search Engine Optimization offers relevance, trustworthiness as well as authority. The list of prime off page search engine optimization methods include domain level keyword agnostic features, content features, domain level brand features, page level keyword agnostic features and domain level keyword usage. Off page search engine optimization, also called as off site search engine optimization, is important just like on page SEO. Building back links is the most important off page search engine optimization tactic and sites with so many back links will rank better than a site with few back links.

Earning links from external website is the most common search engine optimization strategy and key off page SEO strategies include social media marketing, guest blogging, linked brand mentions and influencer marketing. Off page Search Engine Optimization involves improving search engine and user perception of a site's quality. Off page SEO techniques will help improve the website position in search engine results and creating shareable content is the noted off page SEO tactic. Content is always the king in search engine optimization and creating amazing content is the best search engine optimization strategy. According to world-class web marketing technocrats, the content in a website should be always updated and fresh.

Influencer outreach is a well known off page search engine optimization method and contributing as a guest blogger is another top off page SEO tactic. Social media engagement is another major off page SEO technique and it will be helpful in getting more back links. The list of top social networking sites includes Twitter, Facebook, LinkedIn, Pinterest and Instagram. Social bookmarking sites are the best platforms to promote website content and the list of leading social bookmarking sites include Reddit, Stumble Upon, Digg, Slash Dot, and Techno rati. Directory submission will help a website to get more back links and the list of blog directory sites includes technorati and Blog Adda.

Submitting articles in article directories is an excellent off page search engine optimization tactic. It is important to submit unique and high quality content in article directories like Ezine Articles and Squidoo. Only top quality content should be submitted in article directories since low quality content and content with keyword stuffing will get rejected in prominent article directories. The list of well known key article submission sites includes The Free Library, Mag Portal, Ezine Articles and Hub Pages. One of the best ways to get traffic is from question and answer websites and joining high PR question and answer sites will be highly beneficial.

Video submission is another prominent off page search engine optimization technique and the list of video sharing sites include the one and only YouTube, Vimeo, Daily Motion, and Meta Cafe. Sharing photos on popular image submission websites is a best off page SEO strategy and images should be optimized with correct URL and title tag. Flickr, Instagram, Pinterest, Deviant Art, and Shutterfly are the leading image submission sites. Infographics submission is another frequently used off page search engine optimization technique. It is a good practice to submit Infographics on Infographics submission sites like Visual.ly, Reddit, and Nerd Graph.

Document sharing is another off page SEO method and the best document sharing websites include Slideshare, Scribd and Box. Web 2.0 submission is another great idea for off page search engine optimization and Blogger, Tumblr and WordPress are the classic examples of web 2.0 submissions. Some of the best tips for Web 2.0 submissions include sharing great content, updating the site regularly, and building back link for published article. 'Google My Business' platform can be optimized for local search engine optimization and it should have a proper description with 250 characters. Link building is a part of off page SEO and off page search engine optimization goes beyond link building.

Google takes into account lots of off page SEO factors including links and back links are the most critical part of off page SEO. On page search engine optimization and off page search engine optimization are the wheels of SEO vehicle. Off page SEO factors are not directly controlled by the publisher and the off page search engine optimization is a long term process. Off page search engine optimization works in the background to improve rankings and off page SEO plays an important role in the backend. Social media, video marketing and blogging will help the off page search engine optimization of a website.

Link building is one of the famous ways of doing off site search engine optimization and it is the process of building external links with a website. Some of the link building methods include blog directories, forum signatures, comment links, article directories, shared content directories and link exchange schemes. Mentioning the brand on social media platforms like Facebook, Instagram, Twitter and Pinterest will drive lots of traffic. Social bookmarking is appreciated by search engines since the content in social bookmarking sites is frequently updated. Curating new, unique and compelling content is another well known link building strategy followed by web marketing companies.

Off page SEO consists of video submission, articles, ebook creation, bookmarking, blog posting, classified ad and directory submission. Off page search engine optimization paves the way towards more rankings, more exposure, and better Page Rank. A successful off page search engine optimization strategy will increase website rankings in Google. Off page search engine optimization leads to more clicks, more visits, more links as well as more mentions in social media. Off page SEO is all about link building, social media and local search engine optimization.

The first and foremost objective of off page search engine optimization is creating trust, exposure and brand awareness. Assertive internet marketing professionals say that off page SEO is associated with popularity, quality as well as relevance. Social media helps link building to a large extent and it offers a unique opportunity to get in touch with customers. Engaging customers with interesting content is the big part of off page search engine optimization. It has been reported that local SEO is also off page SEO and off page SEO is an integral part of SEO strategy. Off page SEO supplements on page SEO and both of them work together to produce outstanding results. Off page search engine optimization is tremendously valuable because it tells search engines what the page is about.

Difference between Search Engine Optimization and Search Engine Marketing

Search engine optimization is the process of improving the visibility of a website in search engine results. Search engine marketing is a web marketing tactic that increases site visibility through organic search results. Search engine marketing includes search engine optimization and other search marketing tactics. Search engine optimization is an essential component of search engine marketing and SEO consists of on page SEO and off page SEO. On page SEO includes incorporating keywords, optimizing page load speed, social sharing integration within the content, and Google authorship.

Off page Search Engine Optimization consists of back links, social sharing signals, and social bookmarking. SEM includes the usage of paid search, pay per click listings as well as advertisements. The main difference between search engine optimization and search engine marketing is that SEO is a component of search engine marketing. It is not recommended to use the terms search engine optimization and search engine marketing interchangeably. Search engine optimization and search engine marketing are not the same term although they work hand in hand. Organic SEO is definitely the best approach and SEM can't succeed with organic search engine optimization. There are many situations where PPC makes more sense than search engine optimization and creating PPC campaign takes less time than SEO. Organic search engine optimization takes longer to show results and search engine marketing is an essential marketing strategy for brands.

Search engine optimization and search engine marketing are different approaches to search optimization. Search marketing refers to any tactic that helps a brand get attention by appearing on search engine results pages. SEM makes use of paid strategies to appear in search and SEO uses organic strategies to appear in results. The main difference between SEO and SEM is that SEM is paid strategy whereas SEO is an organic strategy. Search engine marketing is an umbrella term that encompasses both paid and organic strategies.

Search marketing helps a particular brand to increase search visibility, improve search rankings and drive more website traffic. SEM is often referred as paid search or pay per click marketing and Google Ads is the leading SEM platform. Brands don't pay for placement on SERPs with search engine optimization and SEO results are valuable and authoritative. White hat SEO strategies are categorized into on page SEO, technical SEO and off page search engine optimization. The key on page search engine optimization strategies include keyword research, content creation and keyword optimization. On page search engine optimization helps search engines understand the page content better. Technical SEO is related to site speed, mobile friendliness, indexing, crawlability and site architecture.

Technical SEO improves both user and search crawler experience which leads to higher search rankings. According to street smart web marketers, a strong SEO plan is a combination of on page SEO, off page SEO and technical SEO. Search engine optimization and search engine marketing are unique elements of search marketing. Both search engine optimization and search engine marketing help a particular brand to appear in search results. Both search engine marketing and search engine optimization drive more traffic to a website and they target specific keywords.

The first step of both search engine marketing and search engine optimization is performing keyword research. Both search engine optimization and search engine marketing require testing as well as continual optimization. The search results of SEM include 'Ad' designation and the search results of SEO appear as organic results. The results of SEM are immediate whereas the results of SEO will take some time to show results. Search engine optimization provides value over time and the click through rate of Search Engine Marketing is lower. The click through rate of search engine optimization is higher and SEM search results will have 'Ad' extensions. A business brand is charged each time a user clicks on the result and a brand is never charged when a user clicks on an organic result.

SEM results are shown to a selected target audience and the SEM search results are filtered based on age and location. The impact of SEM is immediate whereas the impact of SEO will take some time to show results. SEM is better for testing than SEO and SEO has a higher click through rate than search engine marketing. Search engine marketing is an effective way to drive traffic while building organic search engine optimization. SEO is the process of maximizing the number of visitors to a website and it is one aspect of search engine marketing.

SEM traffic is very important because it is targeted and SEM goes beyond search engine optimization. SEM based advertising activities include targeted ad campaigns, writing copy using selective keywords, and applying key performance indicators like click through rates and cost per click. Search engine marketing is great for brand recognition and it is the best way to bring in targeted traffic to a website. SEM is about getting traffic via paid ads and SEO is more about acquiring and monitoring traffic patterns. Both SEM and SEO rely on keywords to drive traffic to business websites and SEM is meant for targeted ads. Search engine optimization is the foundation for good search engine marketing and both of them lead to high quality traffic.

User experience is more important to SEO than SEM and business organizations are well aware of the fact that search marketing will bring massive amount of traffic to their web properties. Google Ads (Formerly Google AdWords) is the most popular and successful search engine marketing program of today. Strong and dynamic SEM strategy provides better results and it offers the best return on investment. SEO provides high quality leads at a cheaper cost and every online marketer can get benefitted from SEO. SEO of contemporary age is all about content marketing and brands should focus on creating remarkable content.

Building traffic using SEO is not complex as many of the internet marketers may think and businesses will have to invest time and money to get amazing SEO results. Search engine optimization can offer better return on investment when compared with traditional forms of marketing. Content quality ensures better SEO results and businesses should ensure that they are publishing long pieces of content. The basic principle of Search Engine Optimization is that an ideal website should be simple and easy to navigate. Adding relevant images to content is a best SEO practice and Search Engine Optimization features higher sustainability. Publishing quality content on a regular basis is the foundation of search engine optimization and creating content that gets ranked well in search engines is not that easy.

Keyword Research

Keyword research is the process of discovering words and phrases that people use in search engines. The ultimate goal of keyword research is optimizing the content and keyword research affects every SEO task. Content topics, on page Search Engine Optimization, outreach as well as promotion are affected by keyword research. It is a well known fact that keyword research is the first step of any search engine optimization campaign. Keyword research gives a crystal clear idea of what potential customers are searching for and Google and YouTube are the best places to find amazing keywords.

Uber Suggest, SEM Rush and Ahrefs are the best tools for finding the appropriate keywords and all of them save lots of time. Internet marketers should keep in mind that long tail keywords are less competitive and some of the best keyword tools include Moz Keyword Explorer, Google Keyword Planner, Google Trends, and SpyFu keyword research tool. Keyword research tells what people care about, purchasing SEO or inbound marketing software, examining the keywords a website ranks for, creating buyer persona, checking the search volume for keywords, finding similar keywords using SEO software and monitoring change in rankings. Keywordtool.io is a top rated keyword research tool and it has been rated as the best Google Keyword Planner alternative.

Some of the best keyword research tools include Soovle, Jaaxy, Google Search Console, Ahrefs Keyword Explorer, SE Cock Pit, Google Keyword Planner, and Keywords Everywhere. Keywords are an integral part of search engine optimization and the basic foundation of SEO is keyword research. A typical keyword research tool helps an internet marketer to find which keywords work better for a website. Basic keyword research and competitor based keyword research are two types of keyword research. It has been found that competitor based keyword research is more effective and the purpose of keyword research is to find effective keywords.

Some of the prominent keyword research tools are paid and only few of them are absolutely free like Google Keyword Planner. It seems that SEM Rush, Ahrefs, Google Keyword Planner, Long Tail Pro, KW Finder, Spy Fu, and SERP Stat are the most popular keyword research tools. SEM Rush is the best keyword research tool for a typical blogger and it is not just another typical keyword research tool. The SEM Rush gives elaborate information on traffic stats, search engine reports, and Ad Sense CPC. SEM Rush is a highly recommended keyword research tool and Ahrefs keyword explorer tool is one of the widely used keyword research tools. Great user interface makes Ahrefs stand out from other prominent keyword research tools available in the market.

The Google Keyword Planner is one of the most used keyword research tools available today and it is integrated with Google Ads. A Google Ads account is necessary to use the Google Keyword Planner and the unique selling proposition of the Google Keyword Planner is the deep information it offers on Google. The Google Keyword Planner is a good and basic tool for keyword research in search engine optimization. KW Finder is completely dedicated to keyword research and they are one of the rapidly growing web marketing companies. The KW Finder is helpful in finding targeted traffic and more targeted traffic is the final objective of KW Finder.

KW Finder offers both free as well as paid plans and basic plan is the best for smart internet marketers. Long Tail Pro is a cloud based keyword research tool and it is unquestionably one of the most prominent keyword research tools. Spy Fu offers one of the best search engine optimization software available in the market and it helps a brand to stay ahead of the competition. The Spy Fu can be used to get a clear understanding of the competitor's SEO platform and it has several modules including compare websites module, keyword history module, domain history module and related keywords module. Spy Fu offers two basic pricing plans of $79 and $99 per month and it is a solid keyword research product.

Serpstat is a comprehensive keyword research tool and it helps companies to find winning keywords. The Serpstat keyword tool gives the details of search volume, competition, keyword difficulty score and cost per click. There is a detailed keyword difficulty score section in Serpstat and Serpstat is mainly used by small businesses. The Serp Stat has been priced at $19 per month and it continues its unbeatable journey of excellence. Keyword research is at the core of Pay per Click marketing and some of the paid keyword research tools are really worth the money.

WordStream's keyword tool can be used for both Search Engine Optimization and Pay per Click keyword research. Soovle allows internet marketers to explore the most typed in keywords on multiple search engines. Uber Suggest is a prominent free keyword tool and Serp Stat features an all in one search engine optimization platform. Serp Stat has some unique features as a keyword research tool and it is a handy keyword research tool. Keyword research really matters for WordPress and performing keyword research for WordPress is one of the best ways to get in front of more readers. SEO is the main driving force of web content and Yoast SEO is the best plug-in for search engine optimization.

Properly optimizing WordPress site for SEO is not that easy and picking a good web host will be of immense help in the SEO initiatives. Speed is a very important ranking factor for Google and Site Ground is recommended for WordPress hosting. The Google Keyword Planner can be used to research organic keywords by customizing results for competitors. Google Keyword Planner is the best place to start keyword research and KW Finder is a long tail keyword research tool. The Moz Keyword Explorer features relative click through rates of the organic results on a search engine results page.

Keywordtool.io is the great starting point for keyword research and it is free for the first 750+ keyword suggestions. Another elegant feature of Keywordtool.io is that it helps to find long tail keywords for YouTube, Bing, Amazon and the App Store. SEM Rush is a one stop shop for keyword research and it is power packed with variety of features. The SEM Rush gives elaborate information on cost per click, volume, trend, number of results, and ad copies. SEM Rush features regional database for international SEO and Ahrefs is an incredible keyword research tool. According to the information available from the market, the SEM Rush offers fast and efficient results as a keyword research tool.

Search Engine Optimization Ranking Factors

Well optimized website gets more traffic over time and it paves the way towards leads and sales. The most important search engine optimization ranking factors include secure website, page speed, mobile friendliness, domain age, optimized content, technical SEO, user experience, links, social signals as well as real business information. Ranking in SEO refers to the position of the content in search engine results pages and search engine rankings are about the quality of information. Google's search quality ratings check factors like content quality, website information, website reputation, and content creator reputation. The most relevant results are shown in search engine rankings first and secure website refers to website created with well coded website builder, robots.txt file, and sitemap.

According to legendary web marketing professionals, HTTPS is a lightweight ranking factor in Google. Having HTTPS is great for users too and page speed including mobile page speed is considered as one of the key Google ranking factors. Fast loading web pages will improve the user experience and mobile friendliness is another major Google SEO ranking factor. Google's mobile first index has become a reality now and SEO ranking factors lay the foundation for good search engine rankings. Google takes into account different factors like responsive site, large fonts for easy readability, accessibility and navigability.

Authority matters as far as search engine rankings are concerned and ranking factors are usually a combination of great content and off page SEO signals. The domain authority or page authority can be checked using Open Site Explorer and optimized content is a crucial SEO ranking factor. Optimized content is one of the most important search engine ranking factors along with user experience and links. It is important to use keywords in content and fresh and original content is always best for search engine optimization. Duplicate content is a negative SEO ranking factor and it is a good SEO practice to use latent semantic keywords.

It has been pointed out that content optimization consists of optimizing for questions and natural language searches. Keyword stuffing will hurt SEO rankings and content length is a Search Engine Optimization ranking factor. Research has shown that content above 2000 words gets top ten positions in the highly competitive Google search rankings. Longer content attracts more links as well as shares, other two important search engine ranking signals. Video marketing can be used to improve SEO rankings and video should be necessarily included in the content strategy. The keyword phrases should be used in page titles and header tags can be used to show content hierarchy.

Google uses more than 200 ranking factors in their algorithm and they can be categorized into domain factors, page level factors, site level factors, back link factors, special Google algorithm rules, brand signals, on site web spam factors and off site web spam factors. Domain age is a ranking factor in Google and having the keyword in domain acts as a relevance signal. A domain that starts with target keyword will get indexed well in search engines and a keyword appearing in the sub domain can boost rankings. Title tag remains a pivotal on page search engine optimization ranking signal and Google doesn't use the Meta description tag as a ranking factor. Description tag can impact click through rate and click through rate is a key ranking factor as far as Google is concerned.

Content length is correlated with search engine results pages and keyword density is another ranking factor in major search engines. Web pages that cover a topic in-depth get indexed well in search engines like Google, Yahoo and Bing. Bing uses page speed as a ranking factor and identical content on the same site will negatively influence search engine rankings. Having a keyword appearing in the first 100 words of page content is interrelated to Google first page rankings. Outbound link quality and outbound link theme are two crucial Google search engine ranking factors.

Proper grammar and spelling is a quality signal as far as Google search engine rankings are concerned. It is a well known fact that content copied from another web page won't rank well and it won't get indexed at all. According to insider web marketers, images, videos and other multimedia elements affect Google search engine rankings. Excessively long URLs will affect the visibility of a website in search engine results and short URLs have a competitive edge in Google search results. Keyword in URL is another relevance signal in Google search engine rankings and Google prefers content with bulleted lists and numbers.

Presence of sitemap, site up time, server location, breadcrumb navigation, mobile optimization, site usability, use of Google Analytics, and user reviews are other prime Google search ranking factors. It is an undisputable fact that YouTube videos get preferential treatment in Google Search Engine Results Pages. YouTube traffic increased significantly after Google Panda update and not all Google search ranking factors are equally important. H1 tag is another key relevant factor and the keyword should be used in the page copy. Google looks for authoritative content and image optimization positively affects search engine optimization. Google algorithm prefers freshly updated content and a sitemap helps search engines to index pages on the site.

The number of linking domains, the number of linking pages, domain authority of linking page, link relevance, authority of linking domain, and linking from home page are the off page SEO ranking factors. The number of domains linking to the website is one of the most important ranking factors and the number of linking pages is another ranking factor. Content of a page is the most important on page SEO ranking factor and good content must supply a demand. Good content should be linkable and title tag is the most important SEO factor after page content. Ideal content pages should be specific to a given topic and an ideally optimized web page links back to category page.

The search algorithm of Google is incredibly smart and it is changing constantly in order to prevent black hat SEO tactics. User experience is the big priority of Google along with the creation of quality content and adding a blog to website will improve its search engine rankings. Purposeful keyword usage is another key Google search ranking factor and back links are the bread and butter of SEO. Social shares like Facebook likes, tweets, and Pinterest pins influence Google search engine rankings. Social media has a positive impact on the SEO efforts of an organization and mobile usability has become an absolute must now.

THANK YOU!

If you enjoyed this book or benefitted from it anyway, then I would like to ask you for a favour: would you be kind enough to leave a review for this book on Amazon.com? It would be greatly appreciated.

Other Books by MAHINROOP PM

Mega Book of Website Designing

Blogging Masterclass Package 2018

Big Book of Vatakara

Web Marketing Super Course

www.ingramcontent.com/pod-product-compliance
Lightning Source LLC
Chambersburg PA
CBHW071257050326
40690CB00011B/2436